# WALK INTO YOUR NEW

(Transitioning from Mourning to Joy)

*Paula Canady Anderson 2022*

PAULA CANADY ANDERSON, MHS

*Cousin Pauline,
When I think of strong & resilient women, I think of you & Mommy. Thank you for always showing me the way. Keep the faith!
Love, Paula*

Walk Into Your New: Transitioning from Mourning to Joy

Copyright © 2022 by Paula Anderson

All rights reserved. No part of this book may be reproduced or transmitted in any form or by any means without written permission from the author.

ISBN: 979-8-9856372-0-5

Printed in the USA

# PREFACE

While writing this book, my initial focus was the challenge of losing a spouse and living with grief. Immediately, I knew that I had to make peace with grief as it would be my new companion. However, this book is not just for widows and widowers; it is for anyone dealing with loss. It may be the loss of your spouse, sibling, niece, nephew, or friend. The past two years have held losses that will never be forgotten in my family—Karmen, my niece lost to gun violence; Kyle, my nephew, lost to the ravages of sickle cell; Inga, my cousin, lost during the pandemic.

Many people are dealing with losses and wondering how to keep putting one foot in front of the other. I pray this book gives you the push that you need to face another day as you walk into your new. Please note, I do not say new normal because I do not believe it will ever seem normal again.

# DEDICATION

This book is dedicated to my husband, our sons, Darryl and Daniel, and our daughter, Destiny.

Darryl Wayne Anderson

June 13, 1957-August 18, 2020

In our deepest moments of missing you, we are filled with love and gratitude.

You were a good man, a loving man, a strong and steady man—to the end.

# TABLE OF CONTENTS

**PREFACE** ............................................................. I

**DEDICATION** ....................................................... II

**INTRODUCTION** .................................................. V

**GRIEF IS A LIVING THING** ................................... 1

**THE IDIOSYNCRASY OF WIDOWHOOD** ............... 8

**HINDSIGHT IS 2020** ............................................ 13

**SO MUCH TO DO** ............................................... 19

**LET US TALK ABOUT FRIENDS!** ......................... 23

**ARE YOU SLEEPING?** ......................................... 29

**WHAT ABOUT YOU?** .......................................... 36

**PUTTING THINGS IN ORDER** ............................. 43

**BACK TO JOYFUL** ............................................... 49

**THE TABOO TALK** .............................................. 54

**MY AHA MESSAGE** ............................................ 59

**BIBLIOGRAPHY** .................................................. 62

**OTHER RESOURCES** 63

**SAMPLE PAGES** 64

**ACKNOWLEDGMENTS** 68

**ABOUT THE AUTHOR** 70

# INTRODUCTION

*I wrote this book because it is my truth. What is the truth that I would deny? I am a widow. Those words do not roll off my tongue so smoothly. They are valid words, but I do not like the sound they make with the silence that rings so loud in my life. I thought we had more time.*

*Many moons ago, we stood—my darling and I before our family, friends, and a church full of people. We uttered those familiar promises to be there in sickness and in health, for better for worse, richer and poorer, till death do us part. We made the vows, and we did it all together—except for dying. Thirty-three years of togetherness, and now I am alone. I am still here. My task is to carry on being the keeper of the flame in our family.*

*We speak of grief as some light and passing thing, but it is neither. It is not linear with a beginning and an end. It is circular and seasonal, with many twists, turns, and reminders everywhere. It creeps into the cracks and crevices of your life as you bake cookies or listen to music. There are hundreds of little reminders each day of the life that you shared. Sweet times, challenging times, the voice you will not hear anymore, the hand you cannot hold, or glances that will no longer be shared across the room.*

*Some think that there are stages to grief—anger, denial, bargaining, depression, and acceptance. It is not the same for everyone. The finality of it sometimes is too hard to bear. I wrote this book so that we might walk together out of the darkness of the grave and into the light of the garden.*

*"He healeth the broken in heart, and bindeth up their wounds."*

Psalm 147:3 KJV

# Grief is a Living Thing

*"Grief is the last act of love we have to give to those we loved. Where there is deep grief, there was great love."*

~Jan Werner

*"The depth of our grief measures the height of our love."*

~ Jan Werner

---

IN THE LATE 1960S, KUBLER-ROSS FOCUSED on dying patients and interviewed them to identify the "the stages of death and dying." (Creagan, 1993). Although I had heard about the five stages of grief before, I just realized it was about the person dying. Kubler-Ross described the stages of grief as denial, bargaining, anger, depression, and acceptance.

I understand now that grief sometimes begins long before death; it starts with the diagnosis. Denial is "the failure to acknowledge an unacceptable truth or emotion or to admit it into consciousness," used as a defense; this stage is characterized by "disbelief" (Creagan, 1993). We think, "I cannot believe this is happening to me." We heard the surgeon's reports, but we still did not believe this was real. We prayed, and then we went to lunch.

Say it is not so…my loved one is asleep and not gone forever. I imagine a different outcome; an alternate reality where my dear loved one is alive and well. In an alternate reality, the accident did not happen. In an alternate reality, there was no cancer or sickness. In an alternate reality, my loved one is healthy and still alive.

Bargaining is another stage of grief. If only I could make a deal with God. If you heal my husband and take this cancer away, I will do WHATEVER you want me to do. If you heal my child or keep them safe, I will do WHATEVER you want me to do. That is a desperate cry. We want to deal with God even though we know that is not how death works.

Anger is the third stage of grief, and we all understand it. We are mad, and there must be someone to blame. Did the doctor make a mistake? Why didn't they find this sooner? People act out this anger with poor behavior—drinking, drugs, etc.

Grief can lead to depression, and this is characterized by sadness. There is little hope for the future: low energy levels and a loss of interest in life. Often you will notice weight loss or weight gain. Some people retreat to their bed and sleep all day while others strike out.

Acceptance occurs when the disease has progressed and is apparent to the patient and the family. The dying person begins to have conversations about their death with their loved ones. It seems that as soon as the patient becomes resolved, the loved ones become more desperate.

Have you traveled through these stages? I certainly have found myself in the deep caverns of despair since my husband's death in 2020. Grief is unique to each person, and they experience it on their own terms. We do not experience these stages in any particular order or over a defined period.

Grief has a life of its own. It tiptoes in at the most inopportune times—at the grocery store, at the park, at family gatherings. Suddenly, sadness washes over you. It is right there, standing alongside the love. You love; therefore, you grieve.

In addition to stages, a quick Google search revealed different types of grief. Who knew that there were stages and types of grief? Yes, there are several types of grief: normal, anticipatory, complicated, chronic, delayed, distorted, prolonged, and collective. This list is not exhaustive, but it is a good start.

*Normal grief* is to experience longing, crying, sadness, despair, insomnia, confusion, disorganized thoughts, disbelief, and many other symptoms.

Normal is detailed with progress towards acceptance and return to basic daily activities.

*Anticipatory grief* is when a loved one is terminally ill and expected to die. Allow the feelings to help you prepare for what is to come. Try to create memorable moments.

*Complicated grief* is intense. It is a constant state of mourning, keeping you from healing. The focus is on death and persistent longing. People in this grief have a hard time enjoying life or being optimistic about their memories.

*Chronic grief* is extreme distress over the loss, and there is no progress. People dealing with this grief are characterized by extended bouts of sadness and severe despair. There is no progress towards feeling better or being more productive.

*Delayed grief* is when the griever avoids the pain of the loss. The sadness and pain are suppressed until long after the person's death.

*Prolonged grief* is incapacitating. The griever experiences prolonged and intense reactions while contemplating the life of the person they have lost. They have not adjusted to life without their loved ones, and they are longing to be with them.

*Collective grief* is felt by the community or a select group when a loss event occurs. Mass shootings and national tragedies fall into this category. The worldwide reaction to the death of George Floyd would be another example of this.

Grief sometimes leaves us with a hangover—exhaustion, puffy eyes, hoarse voice, and an aching heart. Time does not heal, but it may soften the wounds or the loss (Johnson, 2021). Check out the list of symptoms on the next page. Do you recognize any of your symptoms? Circle or underline those that you have experienced. Maybe you have some new things to add.

I have survived this and other losses, but there is no return to normal or the new normal. I will emerge from grief, and I will be forever changed. Looking at this list of common symptoms (Devine, 2021), it all makes sense now. I found a description of myself on this list. How about you?

## *Symptoms of Grief*

| | |
|---|---|
| Insomnia | Trouble concentrating |
| Physical Exhaustion | Hard time reading |
| Time loss | Short attention span |
| Anger | Hypersensitivity |
| Clumsiness | Phantom aches and pains |
| Sleeping all the time | Interpersonal challenges |
| Anxiety | Inability to cry |
| Nightmares | Numbness |
| Intense dreams | Mood swings |
| Loss of appetite | Crying so hard you gag |
| Loss of interest | Loneliness |
| Eating everything | Memory loss |
| Frustration | Screaming in the car |
| Sense of unreality | Stomach pains |
| Sadness | Chest pains |
| Headache | Confusion |

## REFLECTIONS:
## REFLECT ON THE CHAPTER

## ACTIONS:
### WHAT ACTIONS DO YOU NEED TO TAKE?

*"These things I have spoken unto you, that in me ye might have peace. In the world ye shall have tribulation: but be of good cheer; I have overcome the world."*

John 16:33 KJV

# THE IDIOSYNCRASY OF WIDOWHOOD

**THE DEATH OF A SPOUSE FEELS** like a loss of ourselves. We must sort it out and accept that part of us will never be the same. We have taken a hit. Confusion and panic creep in with the grief. *Widow.* The word itself is dreadful, as it has no synonym, only a definition. It has a color: black (Genevieve Davis Ginsburg, 1995). There are many things to do during the first weeks—the widow must be a part of the planning, not just watching. The worst is over with the funeral, or so everyone thinks. In the weeks to follow, the emotions bubble to the surface, and there may be an eruption. It is time to deal with fears and anxieties.

In those first few months, my eyes would pop open at 5:30 AM as if my husband, DARRYL, were saying "Good Morning" and checking on me. I would look around the room and think of him. I would peacefully lay my head back down on the pillow. I would go into the bedroom and smell my husband's cologne; I thought it was just my imagination. Later, I discovered that my children were coming in and spraying the fragrance because it reminded them of their dad.

"WIDOWSYNCRASY," while it is not a real word, describes the idiosyncrasies and peculiar actions of the widow. Indecisiveness is a hallmark of widowhood. "It is normal to feel insecure about suddenly being in charge after years of team playing" (Genevieve Davis Ginsburg, 1995, p. 37). Most widows need time to find an uncluttered brain to make wise decisions. In the process, they must also allow themselves to make mistakes. I made decisions with my husband in the past, and now, I must learn to make them alone.

Managing my husband's belongings was a part of my grieving process. His watches, favorite shirts, and jacket remain in our bedroom. I have kept his model planes, Eagles paraphernalia, and other trinkets from his childhood. I decided to drive my husband's car and get rid of mine. His car is black, shiny, and classic, just like him. Yes, sometimes I sleep in his t-shirts, and I find comfort in watching a western now and then on Saturday afternoons, just like he did. There is still one closet that I have not touched— not ready for that yet.

Every day, the widow receives mail that serves as a reminder that their spouse is no longer here. The mail will read 'deceased' or 'estate of' and then your spouse's name. Hold the mail, please! Answering the mail and responding on time—oh my. I would write the checks to pay the bills and then not mail them on time. They would be in the bottom of my purse or the car somewhere. Whew! What a mess! I finally set up AUTOPAY.

Etiquette says to respond to gifts and acts of kindness within one month. I failed there too! I purchased special thank you cards and wrote them out, only to lose them in the house somewhere. I found them almost 12 months later and mailed them with my Christmas cards. I needed to complete the task. I was grateful to the friends and family who sent cards, flowers, and gifts. I can only imagine what people must have thought when they received the thank you card and a Christmas card in the same week. Charge it to my head and not to my heart.

**Genevieve Davis** Ginsburg (1995) noted, "some widows go through a running stage. They stay on the go because it is easier to be away from home than to be at home" (p. 14). This was my coping method. In the first year and a half, I went to Florida twice, Michigan and Pennsylvania. Family and friends would comment, "You are getting around." They did not know that I was running. Eventually, I had to make peace with being at home without my husband.

# REFLECTIONS:
## REFLECT ON THE CHAPTER

## ACTIONS:
## WHAT ACTIONS DO YOU NEED TO TAKE?

*Hindsight*

"But I would not have you to be ignorant, brethren, concerning them which are asleep, that ye sorrow not, even as others which have no hope. For if we believe that Jesus died and rose again, even so them also which sleep in Jesus will God bring with him."

1 Thessalonians 4:13-14 KJV

# CHINDSIGHT IS 2020

*"Our memories of our loved ones are the pearl we form around the grain of grief that causes us pain."* ~Jeff Zentner

---

YOU WILL ALWAYS HAVE MEMORIES, AND IN hindsight, you remember the forgotten details. The big picture, minute details, and even the struggles are part of your memories. Sometimes, surprising details flood my memories. I treasure our moments and the family that we built together. Taking the time to reflect revealed nuggets of truth about the love and beauty of our marriage. It also brought a new appreciation for qualities I had come to expect and take for granted.

My husband, Darryl, was a quiet man—the strong, silent type. Like E.F. Hutton, "when he spoke, everyone listened" because he did not waste words. He was a man of velvet and steel. He was tender, compassionate, and strong at the same time. He lived a quiet and intentional life. He was steady, dependable, and oh so consistent. He enjoyed his solitude and protected his downtime.

He loved his family, and what a great legacy that is. We are blessed with so many warm, humorous, and loving recollections of him—at work and play. His love language was acts of service. He was able to fix anything and everything that broke around the house. He tinkered the cars, fixed the washer, replaced the faucets, and he was the whole geek squad when it came to tech or computer problems. Yes, he was that guy!

When Darryl became ill, things changed. He was no longer able to fix everything. His energy was spent on other things. After his death, I noted the many things that had gone ignored over time—repairs to the shed, dripping faucets, and fences that needed mending. It has taken a team of contractors, plumbers, and electricians to get our little house back together.

We were married 33 years, and we lived in our home for 27 of those years. Our home is one big memory box of our life together. We raised our three children in this home. There are photographs everywhere depicting our lives together. In the dining room sits the vase that held the last bouquet of flowers that my husband had delivered to me on my birthday.

Remembering our loved ones becomes the intersection of grief, humor, pain, loss, history, love, and joy. (Hebb, 2018) Even as we call forth loving memories, we must face the loss once more. I often want to say, excuse me, I am not myself. My person has died, and I am not the same. I might cry.

I heard people tell stories about my husband days after his death and during his homegoing service. They had special memories of him. They spoke of their love for him, their admiration for how he lived his life, and how he loved his family. He was diligent about his work, and he was a kind man. As I listened to his nieces, cousins and coworkers share their stories about him, I thought—he would have loved to know that they thought so highly of him. I wished he knew the depth of his friends and family's love for him. He was a quiet man, but I know he would have appreciated hearing those things during the darker days when he was not feeling well.

We were home together during Covid, and that brought comfort. We had our meals together, laughed together, and watched old movies together. There were difficult conversations as we faced an uncertain future. Darryl's death brought me face to face with my own mortality. We know that tomorrow is not promised, but we often live like we have so much time.

Let us make sure that we tell our people that we ***LOVE*** them. If you love somebody, tell them. Let them know that they are important to you every chance you get. Do not let them wonder if you appreciate them; TELL ***THEM.***

In hindsight, my 20/20 vision is LOVE. As we fully grieve our loss, we once again appreciate all the beautiful things about our loved one—falling in love all over again. We find ourselves, once again, enchanted by their gifts (Hebb, 2018). We had a love that would last forever in my heart. He was my guy, and I was his girl! We knew it from the very beginning. I wish we had more time. He was a man of strong convictions and character. He loved God and family. I see him in our three children—the adults that have risen to call me blessed. I was and still am a BLESSED woman. I do not know what the future holds, but I know that God holds my future. There may be lonely times, but I am not alone.

## REFLECTIONS:
## REFLECT ON THE CHAPTER

## ACTIONS:
## WHAT ACTIONS DO YOU NEED TO TAKE?

*"Fear thou not; for I am with thee: be not dismayed; for I am thy God: I will strengthen thee; yea, I will help thee; yea, I will uphold thee with the right hand of my righteousness."*

Isaiah 41:10 KJV

# SO MUCH TO DO

---

**THERE IS SO MUCH TO DO WHEN** a loved one dies, whether it is your parent, spouse, or child. The widow/widower, especially, has many responsibilities. When your spouse passes, there are many questions and many decisions to be made. All eyes are on you for the answers.

When my husband died, I realized that although we had reluctantly discussed a few things, it was not enough in hindsight. My husband had cancer, and we spent many days having faith-filled and hopeful conversations. As the disease progressed, we discussed hospice and his wishes regarding his do not resuscitate order (DNR) and power of attorney for health (POA). He did not spend much time speaking about his death. He talked to our adult children about life and taking care of each other. My husband was at home on hospice care; he died at home.

Once he passed, I knew who would officiate and give remarks. Everything else was a blur, and time seemed to stand still. My husband died during the pandemic; therefore, the plans for his funeral and gathering for a repast were impacted by safety and health practices, limiting the number of people allowed to gather. This was difficult as my husband was one of seven children, and there were many friends and ministry partners. It made for a very intimate gathering of family and a few special friends.

Honestly, I felt tremendous pressure to do things in a manner that would bring honor to the life that he led. I gave myself a moment and took a breath. On the day of my husband's death, I decided to do one thing and tabled the rest for another day. I selected the mortuary that would handle his remains, and they came to the house. After that, I needed to breathe, and maybe you do too! There were so many things left to do.

At the time of death, many things are needed to plan a funeral/farewell tribute for your loved one. You will want to honor the memory of the life that they lived. Perhaps you had a conversation outlining final wishes, including clear-cut directions, or maybe you didn't know where to begin. Managing your sadness and fear about what is to come while emotionally supporting your children and close family members is a humongous task.

**Contact the important people:**

- Family—parents, children, siblings, and extended family
- Employer/Human Resources to discuss benefits; death benefits, health, and disability, retirement accounts
- Other business—wills, trusts, probate
- Bank documents—close/transfer ownership of bank accounts
- Update beneficiaries on insurance policies

When I went through the documents and made the calls, I felt extreme pressure to make the right decisions. It was incredibly stressful because I did not want to make the wrong decision. Before my husband died, I was confident in my choices. I was accustomed to bouncing ideas off my husband. Suddenly, I had to decide on my own—another reminder that I was alone.

I sought counsel from a few trusted people, then moved forward. I spoke with an attorney, a banker, a tax advisor, and an estate planner. They all had advice for me, and I used collective wisdom to make the best decisions for my family. I prayed to the Father for wisdom, and then I proceeded forward. You will do the same.

My advice to you is this—do not feel rushed into decisions. Be gentle with yourself, allowing time for your emotions to settle down. Do not make major decisions in that first year. In other words, do not sell your house; do not move to another state; do not quit your job, etc. Let those decisions simmer until you are more settled into your new life situation. Be kind to your grieving self.

Leave the dishes in the sink sometimes, take a day off when you need it, stay in bed, or do nothing sometimes. Cry when you want to, or do not cry if you do not want to.

Grief is personal and unique to every individual. There is no timeframe—no ought to. No one can tell you if it is too much or too little. My favorite piece of nonsense is when people say, "You should be over it by now!" There is no such thing as being over it! Grief remains.

Fight! Fight! Fight to grieve in your own time and your own way!

**Cry**

**Laugh**

**Sit silently**

**Spend time with others**

**Spend time alone**

**Rise early**

**Rise late**

**Stay in bed all-day**


And whatever else you need to do.

*"Two are better than one; because they have a good reward for their labour. For if they fall, the one will lift up his fellow: but woe to him that is alone when he falleth; for he hath not another to help him up."*

*Ecclesiastes 4:9-10 KJV*

# LET US TALK ABOUT FRIENDS!

*"A friend loveth at all times."* ~Proverbs 17:17

---

S O, LET US TALK ABOUT YOUR FRIENDS. They will call and check on you from time to time. You will be swamped in that first week or so. Maybe even the first month if you have a tight circle. Please try to accept the invitations that come because they will fall off as people get back to their lives. You will need to get back to your life also.

There are those surprises that also come at the hands of your friends. People will try to introduce you to their single friends or assume you want to meet other widows/widowers. I will let you know when I am ready to meet someone in a dating capacity. No matchmaking, please! There are those tiny hurtful things that people do unintentionally, or at least you hope it was not intentional. People are sometimes insensitive, and they want you to be better before you are ready.

As I was writing this chapter, I recalled a recent conversation with a relative about an anniversary party for mutual friends. She mentioned that the anniversary party was a lovely event. A year ago, I would have been invited to that party. I was silent, but my heart felt the sting. I can be in the company of married people without my husband. I will not be going to any couple's retreats, but please do not exclude me from our regular gatherings.

I used to be a part of that group of couples. You know, the few who gather for dinner occasionally. I wondered if that meant I would no longer be invited to the couple's gatherings, the brunches, and trips to the beach. Would I be invited to the holiday gathering? Did I just slip their mind, or was it intentional? Did they think it would make me too sad to see other couples? Maybe that is it! I will say my feelings were hurt. Once again, I was reminded that I was alone. No plus one! When the widow walks in, does it remind

We need our friends. Sometimes we do not know how to ask for the help we so desperately need. If you are the friend of someone experiencing great loss, just be there. Be the friend—make the calls, extend the invitations, and pray for them. Do not just say you will do something, DO IT.

Grief leaves you feeling incredibly lonely, and survival is the long haul. Who is there for you, with calls, texts, outings (dinner and movie dates)? I am so incredibly grateful for my family and the friends who have become family. I learned that from my mother, an only child with lots of extended family.

My two sons and daughter have come alongside and have been my emotional support. Not one special day or family time has been missed. My sisters have been Zooming with me almost daily, which has been a cheerful part of my day. I have a circle of friends that are thoughtful and kind. I have a few longtime friends and a few new friends who have made it their business to call me regularly to check in. I am blessed with REAL friends who call my name in prayer and have not forgotten me. I know this because I feel the strength of their love and prayers for me. I thank God every time I think of them.

Many widows speak about being excluded from family events. Some even report that they are no longer invited to weddings, baby showers, and holiday parties. They see the pictures on social media and do not understand why they were left out. I am grateful that my relationship with my in-laws has remained intact. They have been very thoughtful, and our gatherings remain very intentional. A family group chat includes my husband's six siblings, and we still get together during holidays as usual.

How do you move on after the death of your spouse or significant other? You move on by taking one step at a time. You will sometimes require help or a shove in the right direction. Your friends and family will sometimes provide that necessary shove. It is also important for you to be proactive in this area. Keep in touch with your people (family, friends, social and religious organizations) and make plans to attend your annual events if possible. There will be many yearly events that you now face alone—family gatherings, holiday gatherings, worship services. Make tentative plans to attend. As the time arrives, you may change your mind or choose to attend and stay just a short while. Remember, take steps to stay engaged with your people.

## PAULA CANADY ANDERSON

Everyone is different, and your response may vary depending on the day. I find comfort with old friendships and forging new friendships. It is crucial to do both. I welcome opportunities to see old friends and family, but I also welcome new relationships and opportunities. I stretch myself to do new things and find new connections. It is important to say "yes" to life and living.

## REFLECTIONS:
## REFLECT ON THE CHAPTER

## ACTIONS:
## WHAT ACTIONS DO YOU NEED TO TAKE?

*"But thou, O Lord, art a shield for me; my glory, and the lifter up of mine head. I cried unto the Lord with my voice, and he heard me out of his holy hill. Selah. I laid me down and slept; I awaked; for the Lord sustained me."*

Psalm 3:3-5 KJV

# Are You Sleeping?

**A**RE YOU SLEEPING? THE SHORT ANSWER TO this common question is "No!" If I am honest, sleep escapes me 2-3 nights a week. People ask and offer solutions that sometimes work. Some people resort to medication, others to alcohol with different and inconsistent results. No one has the answers to the questions asked in the darkness.

During an early conversation with my Pastor, he asked the question. I gave him the short and sweet answer, "Sometimes I sleep through the night." He suggested that I try sleeping on my husband's side of the bed. Late one night, around 2 AM, weary and exhausted, I tried laying on his side of the bed. I was pleasantly surprised to find comfort. My reward was a peaceful night's sleep. Now, his side of the bed has BECOME my side.

It is essential to have a nighttime routine. You must be intentional in your efforts to end your evening activities. The television, screen time, and telephone conversations need to end one to two hours before retiring to the bedroom. Strive to turn the lights out early enough to get a good night's sleep—at least 8 hours. I sleep best in a dark room that is not too hot.

If I am still walking around at midnight, chances are I will still be awake at 2 AM or 3 AM. Facebook and Instagram let me know that I am not alone. People are awake playing games and reading comments into the wee hours of the early morning. In addition to a good nighttime routine, I have found the weighted blanket helpful. Truth be told, I am still working on my morning and evening routines, exercise routines, and self-care. It all begins with restful sleep.

The body and the mind are replenished and renewed through sleep. Circadian rhythms, controlled by the brain, are the body's natural and internal clock that tells our mind and body to go to sleep and wake up. Circadian rhythms impact mental, physical, and behavioral processes. They also affect your appetite, hormones, temperature, blood pressure, sleep, and melatonin levels (Figure 1).

**Figure 1**

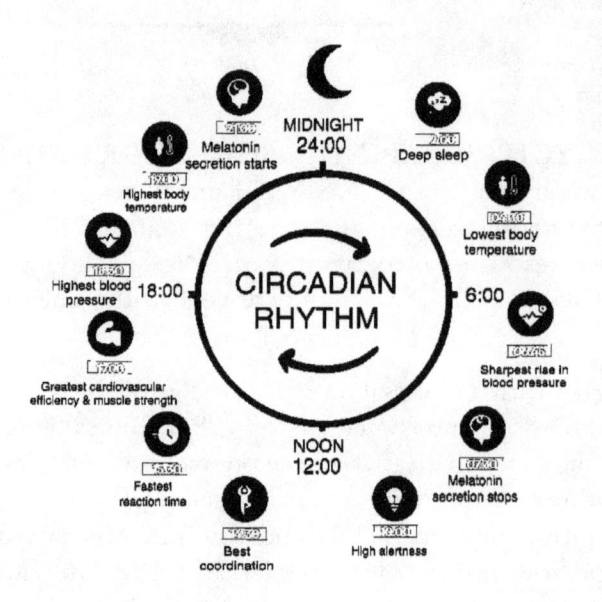

*Note*: Adapted from S. Waters (2021)

Here are some factors that impact Circadian Rhythms:

- Artificial light from the television and telephone screens
- Stress and hormones (fight or flight)
- Noise
- Caffeine
- Health
- Medication
- Exercise
- Work schedules (graveyard shifts)

When the Circadian rhythms are uncoordinated, the following problems may result—insomnia, bowel issues, and brain fog. These are some ways to reset your rhythms:

- Reduce alcohol and caffeine
- Take naps
- Turn off the gadgets when preparing for bed
- Stay hydrated – water is best
- Consider using a Happy Light (Verilux)

## WALK INTO YOUR NEW

| *What helps me SLEEP?* | *What keeps me AWAKE?* |
|---|---|
|  |  |

What is your sleep routine?

_____
_____
_____
_____
_____
_____
_____

## REFLECTIONS:
## REFLECT ON THE CHAPTER

## ACTIONS:
## WHAT ACTIONS DO YOU NEED TO TAKE?

*"Nay, in all these things we are more than conquerors through him that loved us. For I am persuaded, that neither death, nor life, nor angels, nor principalities, nor powers, nor things present, nor things to come, Nor height, nor depth, nor any other creature, shall be able to separate us from the love of God, which is in Christ Jesus our Lord."*

Romans 8:37-39 KJV

# What About You?

PEOPLE ASK, "HOW ARE YOU DOING?" and keep walking. Some will pause long enough for you to answer. So, how are you? Really! Self-care must be your priority. Are you spending a large portion of the day making sure everyone else is good? We are often responsible for taking care of others—parents, spouse, children, etc. We often cater to the needs of those around us without thinking of ourselves. Are you hungry? Thirsty? Can I do anything for you? Even in our grief, there are responsibilities.

What about you? What do you need? Stop, take a moment, and think about yourself. It is not selfish to care for oneself. Do you need a break? Take one. Do you need to rest? Take a nap or plan a getaway. Are you playing music? Are you free to dance to the music at least once a day? Are you feeling stressed? Aching neck and shoulders? You should schedule a massage. Take the time to consider your needs and schedule some downtime.

Are you eating? Let us just acknowledge that there is just no fun cooking for one person or eating alone. Cereal was the dinner choice on occasion. Widows binge and overeat, becoming fat and fluffy, and others do not eat enough and lose weight. Just one look, and you know I have been eating! There were many take-out options from Chinese to pizza and burgers in that first year. I eventually had to change that pattern and return to healthier eating. It is essential to eat a balanced diet. Be intentional about your meals. Cook and freeze simple meals in single-serving sizes. So, when you are ready to eat, you can go to your freezer and get a healthy meal. Wholeness and health are your responsibility.

Grief is exhausting and leaves you spent. Sleepless nights and tearful days leave you drained. It is vital to allow time to refresh. Spend time with the people you love and those who bring positive energy to your life. You are worth the time and effort. Planned care is essential, especially when facing difficult appointments and challenging times.

I have learned to plan for times of renewal. Take quarterly breaks and spend weekends away with your family or friends. I enjoy the company of friends and family. Laughter is always welcome. I try to include time at the beach or poolside to relax. Let us not forget to throw in some tasty food, lively conversation, and maybe a massage. I return home feeling lighter, weights lifted, and ready to face another day.

Be intentional as you create your landscape for activities that bring comfort to you. You might try journaling, preparing a vision board, or writing a letter to your future self.

**Make daily preparation for self-care activities:**

- Morning Prayer – prepare your Bible and journal for morning meditation.

- Take a walk – lay out your jogging suit, sneaks, headphones, and set your alarm to rise early.

- Afternoon tea - set up your tea kettle, candle, favorite mug, and fabulous tea, of course.

- Reading - set up a relaxing station with a comfortable chair, good lighting, and a warm throw.

Here are a few other things that I have tried to encourage fun and relaxation:

- Gardening
- Line Dancing
- Road Trips
- Walking
- Museum Trips
- Yoga
- Podcasts
- Take a nap
- Movies
- Go to the beach
- Try new recipes
- Read a book
- _____
- _____
- _____
- _____

Megan Devine suggests that you write your own **Personal Manifesto** and take the time to evaluate your feelings whenever you are trying new things. Note how you felt, what you wanted, what you chose, and what happened when you did. How are you feeling today?

Remember to also plan for self-care around difficult times such as holidays, anniversaries, birthdays, or appointments with the lawyer. Set a timer when doing complex tasks (i.e., reading the will). Schedule a movie with friends. Treat yourself kindly. Validate yourself and find ways to manage the intense emotions. Breathe! Sometimes all we can do is breathe.

Breathing is essential to our self-care. "Studies in both trauma sciences and neurobiology show that lengthening your exhale helps soothe the nervous system when it's agitated, as it is when you're feeling acute anxiety. This simple action stops the flood of stress hormones that trigger escalating anxiety" (Devine, 2021, p. 63).

And what about your SURVIVAL? Say yes to more; say no to more; participate in nourishing things; get out of the door; seek out new ideas. What is your RIGHT NOW list of things that need your attention?

What are the other self-care directives? How about that annual physical? Dental and vision examinations? Get busy scheduling your routine check-ups and follow-up examinations. Take the necessary steps to be healthy and strong—physically, mentally, and spiritually.

Grief counseling was also a part of my self-care. The weekly Zoom calls were a great help during that first year after my husband's death. It was offered through the hospice organization that worked briefly with my husband during his illness. This door remains open if I should ever need to talk to someone. If counseling is available to you, take advantage of the offer. It will be beneficial for you and your family.

## REFLECTIONS:
## REFLECT ON THE CHAPTER

## ACTIONS:
## WHAT ACTIONS DO YOU NEED TO TAKE?

*"But the Comforter, which is the Holy Ghost, whom the Father will send in my name, he shall teach you all things, and bring all things to your remembrance, whatsoever I have said unto you. Peace I leave with you, my peace I give unto you: not as the world giveth, give I unto you. Let not your heart be troubled, neither let it be afraid."*

John 14:26-27 KJV

# Putting Things in Order

*"A good man leaveth an inheritance to his children's children: and the wealth of the sinner is laid up for the just." Proverbs 13:22 KJV*

---

NOW, LET US GET STARTED ON those things that are a little more practical when someone dies. If you are the spouse, chances are you were the named beneficiary. Thus, you are responsible for insurance policies, bank accounts, property, or other assets that must be handled. Make sure your legal affairs are in order. Do this because your heirs deserve organized and efficient paperwork!

You need to know where to go and whom to speak to when you put things in the proper order. The first document you need is the death certificate. Most banks and insurance companies require an official death certificate to handle any transactions. Some may also require a marriage certificate and possibly additional information to move forward. There may be accounts that you need to close to ensure that there are no opportunities for fraud or identity theft.

Contact your spouse's employer/human resource department to discuss employee benefits. They will discuss any policy requirements. Here is the checklist:

- Last Will and Testament – contact your attorney to discuss the will and any needed actions or updates. Some states will require probate of the will.

- Life insurance — death benefits, retirement plans, and other outstanding issues.

# WALK INTO YOUR NEW

Contact your insurance agent to update beneficiary information. Contact your bank to update beneficiaries and signers to your accounts. Update your will and consider other documents that will assist with managing your remaining estate.

It is important to take care of these details. This is your legacy, and it matters to your family, children, grandchildren, and charitable interests. I want to ensure that my wishes are understood in the event of my death. Your loved ones will appreciate your diligence with this documentation. They deserve good documents!

These are the essential documents. If you do not have these documents, you must put them together immediately.

***Legal identification documents: Keep these records forever.***

- Social security cards
- Birth certificates
- Death certificates
- Marriage certificates
- Tax documents-returns and W-2s (save for seven years)
- Property records
- Vehicle registration
- Medical records

***Consult your attorney about these five legal documents and update them annually:***

- Advanced Medical Directive (living will)
- Durable Power of Attorney for Healthcare
- Durable Power of Attorney for Finance

- Revocable Living Trust
- Last Will and Testament

*Financial records:* list all bank accounts, investment accounts, and beneficiaries.

*Estate planning documents and life insurance documents*: Store the documents in a safe deposit box and ensure that a trusted friend or family member knows where the files are.

*Where are your important papers?*

I know this seems like a lot, but it is well worth your time and effort. Your loved ones will appreciate your diligence with this documentation. If you do not have these documents, GET ORGANIZED NOW!

## REFLECTIONS:
## REFLECT ON THE CHAPTER

## ACTIONS:
### WHAT ACTIONS DO YOU NEED TO TAKE?

*"To walk worthily of the Lord unto all pleasing, bearing fruit in every good work, and increasing in the knowledge of God; strengthened with all power, according to the might of his glory, unto all patience and longsuffering with joy."*

Colossians 1:10-11 ASV

# BACK TO JOYFUL

*"A merry heart doeth good like a medicine, but a broken spirit drieth the bones."*
~Proverbs 17:22 KJV

---

SO, WHO ARE YOU NOW? That is a great question. Over time, you will emerge on the other side of grief. You will make it through the dark times. I am sure you realize that you are changed. You will never be the same. Some days I feel stuck, but I continue to strive towards forwarded movement. I must continue because God has a work for me to do. "I do not understand the mystery of grace—only that it meets us where we are and does not leave us where it found us" (Anne Lamott, *Traveling Mercies*, Johnson, 2021).

Love yourself because it will bring more love into the world. Let's get going! It is crucial to find your way. I am a strong proponent of positive action and vision. I do vision board parties to encourage others to pursue their dreams. I also use vision boards to promote my own dreams and aspirations.

Do you have a vision for your life going forward? You may have children to care for or a demanding career. Let's carve out a concept that allows you to have a work-life balance.

To balance your life, several key areas must be addressed: health and wellness, spiritual, family relationships, social and professional aspects. These key areas need your attention.

- Health and Wellness - Are you getting rest and good exercise? Make time to schedule and keep routine medical examinations.

- Spiritual – What are you feeding your spirit? Worship services? Are you reading or listening to positive and encouraging affirmations?

- Family – Are you honoring family traditions or making new traditions? Annual events and gatherings?

- Social – Are you spending time with friends? Are you meeting new people? Are you visiting new places for entertainment?

- Professional – Pursue your career goals and desires.

Find new ways to bring laughter and love to your life. "Life is built alongside loss, informed by beauty and grace as much as by devastation"(Devine, 2021). We must continue to walk through life with grief and loss as our companions. My life is informed by devastation and joy. It is weaving, a tapestry that has many strands. It has some sadness, loss, anger, and disappointment, but the major strands running through the tapestry of my life are love, joy, peace, strength, and the grace of God. It is complicated. We make our way from mourning to elation. Joy will sometimes feel like a betrayal, but we will continue to live and appreciate each new day because with it comes another chance at joy.

The grace of God has met me in every circumstance, and it has been sufficient for every challenge. He has not left me stranded. He meets me right in the middle of my situation—whether I am lonely, afraid, or anxious about the future. God's love and his grace have sustained me. He is the reason I can face tomorrow!

## REFLECTIONS:
## REFLECT ON THE CHAPTER

## ACTIONS:
## WHAT ACTIONS DO YOU NEED TO TAKE?

*"Finally, brethren, whatsoever things are true, whatsoever things are honest, whatsoever things are just, whatsoever things are pure, whatsoever things are lovely, whatsoever things are of good report; if there be any virtue, and if there be any praise, think on these things. Those things, which ye have both learned, and received, and heard, and seen in me, do: and the God of peace shall be with you."*

*Philippians 4:8-9 KJV*

# THE TABOO TALK

---

OUR TALKS ABOUT DEATH WITH OUR family and friends should occur regularly over dinner. Death is a part of life; therefore, we must not be afraid to talk. Schedule a time to gather, invite your family and tell them you want to talk about death. I witnessed a few such conversations with my great-grandmother and my great-aunt. I was the child sitting quietly in the room as they discussed funeral garb, you know, what color they wanted to be buried in. I remember them talking about staying in their home and not a nursing facility.

Usually, these conversations came up after attending someone's funeral. They would talk about too many flowers or not enough flowers. Mind you, my great-grandmother lived past my college graduation, and my great-aunt Abbey saw me married with children. These conversations occurred so often that I knew what music would be played and who would do the eulogy. She wanted rousing music in the 'celebration' of her life. I wish they had paid as much attention to their legal documents, such as making a will and having powers of attorney for health and finance. I watched my mother struggle to get their affairs in order.

I firmly believe that when you know better, you must do better. If possible, everyone needs to put their affairs in order before dying. It is an act of love to ensure the smooth transition of your estate to your loved ones.

People used to think that only the rich needed a will. Contrary to popular opinion, EVERYBODY needs to have a succession plan. Aging in place is a beautiful idea for many. People want to avoid living in a rehabilitation or hospital setting, so it's critical to speak with your loved ones about care in the home. These talks are better over dinner with everyone present and before sickness or death. It is difficult to make decisions when emotions and anxieties are high.

As I was researching such conversations, I came upon two things which were novel ideas to me, 'death over dinner' and the idea of a 'living funeral.' These two ideas were intriguing to me. There is a whole death-over-dinner movement, but you'll have to research that on your own. The living funeral has two forms. In the first option, the honoree lays in a coffin, and the family and friends conduct a funeral. That is a bit extreme for me. The other practice is simply an elaborate farewell when someone is terminally ill or very old, giving the accolades and celebrating the person while they are alive.

I encourage you to talk to your loved ones and celebrate life while realizing none of us escapes death. As we accept our mortality, we value each day a little differently and love life more fully! Life and death are part of life. This conversation needs to occur, and it is vital to share your thoughts about your life and final wishes.

## REFLECTIONS:
## REFLECT ON THE CHAPTER

## ACTIONS:
## WHAT ACTIONS DO YOU NEED TO TAKE?

*And God will wipe away every tear from their eyes; there shall be no more death, nor sorrow, nor crying. There shall be no more pain, for the former things have passed away. Revelation 21:4 (NKJV)*

# MY AHA MESSAGE

---

CAN I BELIEVE IN THE SOVEREIGNTY OF God and still ask why? Of course, I can, and you can too! Why did I lose my loved ones so soon? It always feels 'too soon.' Why did I lose my dad when he was only forty-nine and my mom at sixty-five? Why, oh why did I lose my husband at sixty-three? We planned to retire, travel, and grow old together, but that was not our future. I do ask why and wonder aloud to God about His timing. I want to accept the will of God. I want to believe that God is working out His perfect plan, but it is sometimes just hard.

One day as I pondered these questions, thinking about prayer and how God hears and answers, I thought about a past, answered prayer. I thought about how my husband suffered a heart attack in 2006 when he was forty-nine years old. His heart function was very weak, and they inserted a defibrillator (pacemaker). The doctor proceeded to discuss his need for a heart transplant. We prayed and thanked God for his healing. He never had another heart attack, and his heart was never shocked by the defibrillator. That was an answer to prayer!

As I remembered those prayers and the fourteen years added to his life, from age 49 to 63, I am grateful for the extra time—2006 until 2020! I thought about the scripture that says, "It is appointed unto man once to die" (NKJV, Hebrews 9:27). I began to think about how God extended Darryl's life for another fourteen years. That was God answering prayer and giving our little family of five the *more* we prayed for—more time, more life, and more love. I am grateful for the trips we were able to take and the milestones he was here to see—growing older together, our children growing up and graduating from high school and college, and moving into adulthood. I am thankful for God's grace towards us!

We pray, but we do not know how God will answer. We cry out for healing and deliverance. We trust that God does not want us to suffer. We have the sweet assurance of life beyond the grave—heaven with no more death, sorrow, pain, or tears. The truth is He answered our prayers for healing. God always heals, but not always on this side of heaven. In faith, we trust God to make us whole again, and He does, on both sides of heaven.

*"For if we live, we live to the Lord, and if we die, we die to the Lord. So then, whether we live or whether we die, we are the Lord's. For to this end, Christ died and lived again, that he might be Lord both of the dead and of the living."* Romans 14:7-9

# BIBLIOGRAPHY

Creagan, T. (1993, February 1). *Psychosocial Issues in Oncologic Practice.* 68,161-167. doi:https://doi.org/10.1016/s0025-6196(12)60164-5

Devine, M. (2021). *How To Carry What Can't Be Fixed: A Journal ForGrief.* Boulder: Sounds True.

Genevieve Davis Ginsburg, M. (1995). *Widow to Widow: Thoughtful, Practical Ideas ForRebuilding Your Life.* New York: Hachette.

Hebb, M. (2018). *Let's Talk About Death (Over Dinner).* New York: Hachette.

Johnson, M. C. (2021). *Finding Refuge: Heart Work For Healing Collective Grief.* Boulder: Shambhala.

Waters, S. (2021, September 14). *How Not To Lose Sleep Over Your Circadian Rhythms.* Better Up Blog. San Francisco, California, West. Retrieved December 27, 2021, from http://www.betterup.com

Werner, J. (2018). *Grief Day ByDay.* Emeryville: Althea Press.

# OTHER RESOURCES

Gerson, M. (2021). *Forget Prayers, Bring Cake: A Single Woman's Guide To Grieving*. San Rafael: Mandala

Orman, S. (2020). *The Ultimate Retirement Guide: Winning Strategies To Make Money Last A Lifetime*. Carlsbad: Suze Orman Media

**Websites**

Terrible, Thanks for Asking

https://www.ttfa.org

The Mindfulness & Grief Podcast with Heather Stang

https://mindfulnessandgrief.com

# Sample Pages

SAMPLE

## POWER OF ATTORNEY FOR HEALTHCARE
## SIMPLE HEALTH CARE DIRECTIVE

This form combines the many different state legal requirements into a "universal" legal form intended to meet the standard requirements in most states. Look for free templates online or contact your attorney. Discuss your wishes and priorities directly with your agent and others who are close to you.

### INFORMATION ABOUT THE PRINCIPAL

Principal's Full Name

Principal's Street Address

City                            State                           Zip Code

Principal's Daytime Phone              Principal's Other Phone

Principal's Date of Birth              Principal's Email Address

### WHO WILL BE YOUR HEALTH CARE AGENT?

Agent's Full Name

Agent's Street Address

City                            State                           Zip Code

Agent's Daytime Phone              Agent's Other Phone

Agent's Email Address

SAMPLE

## LAST WILL AND TESTAMENT

LAST WILL AND TESTAMENT OF _____

I, _____ presently of _____, NJ

Declare that this is my LAST WILL and TESTAMENT.

## PRELIMINARY DECLARATIONS

<u>Prior Wills and Codicils</u>

1. I revoke all prior Wills and Codicils

<u>Marital Status</u>

2. I am in a common law relationship with _____

<u>Current Children</u>

3. I do/do not have any living children.

4. The term 'child' or 'children" as used in this WILL includes the above listed children and any children of mine that are subsequently born or legally adopted.

**EXECUTOR**

<u>Definition</u>

5. The expression "my Executor" used throughout this Will includes either the singular or plural member or the masculine or feminine gender as appropriate wherever the fact or context so requires. The term "executer" in this Will is synonymous with and includes the terms 'personal representative' and 'executrix'

<u>Appointment</u>

6. I appoint my (indicate relationship), _____, as the sole Executor of this my Will

# Monthly Budget Worksheet

| EXPENSES | AMOUNT | DUE DATE | PAID | NOTES |
|---|---|---|---|---|
| HOUSING | | | | |
| | | | | |
| | | | | |
| UTILITIES | | | | |
| | | | | |
| | | | | |
| PHONE/INTERNET | | | | |
| | | | | |
| | | | | |
| GROCERY/HOUSEHOLD ITEMS | | | | |
| | | | | |
| | | | | |
| TRANSPORTATION | | | | |
| | | | | |
| | | | | |
| INSURANCE | | | | |
| | | | | |
| | | | | |
| SAVINGS | | | | |
| | | | | |
| | | | | |
| DEBTS | | | | |
| | | | | |
| | | | | |
| MISCELLANEOUS | | | | |
| | | | | |
| | | | | |

# ACKNOWLEDGMENTS

I am grateful for those who have held me close these past few years.

My babies, Darryl, Daniel, and Destiny—grownups now. Thank you for coming alongside to support me during this transition. Thank you for not missing a birthday, a holiday, or a special date. You made sure that I still get flowers! You have been strong for me while dealing with your own grief and missing Dad. He would be so proud of the adults you are and so happy to see you working together and supporting one another!

My sister-friend, Stephanie, has been a rock for my family and me. Thank you for your strength, love, and willingness to always have my back.

My sisters, Jennifer and Victoria, have kept the laughter coming during our daily video chats. Thank you for making time for me.

My brothers, Joseph, Jeffrey, Lil' Joey, and Robert, who call to check on their big sister!

My sister-friends who hold me up in prayer, Flora, Prudence, Winnie, Darlene, Kim, and Donna—you are precious to me. Your texts in the middle of the day, the group chats, and the PRAYERS. I thank God upon every remembrance of you.

My friend Torri, the author, has encouraged me and spent hours at the bookstore with me. Thank you for sharing your wisdom and letting me pick your brain.

Pastor Joy Morgan and my fellow travelers on the Finish That Book Challenge, thank you for your steady encouragement and reminders that someone needs to read this book. I have met some marvelous people on this journey.

Pastor David G. Evans, I thank you for being a listening ear and for the wisdom that you impart so freely.

Finally, I am most thankful to God, for His mercies are new every morning. He is the Author and Finisher of my faith. In Him, I live, and move, and have my being!

# ABOUT THE AUTHOR

*Paula Canady Anderson, MHS,* is a certified Life Coach and Social Worker in New Jersey. She has over 25 years of experience counseling, training, and facilitating groups in private, government, and community agencies. Paula graduated from Duquesne University and obtained her master's degree at Lincoln University. As the Founder of Livin' On Purpose, LLC, Paula coaches and assists clients in setting goals through vision board work and assists them with various transitions in life.

Paula enjoys dancing, reading, and traveling and has an eclectic taste for music, fashion, and furnishings. She grew up with her mother and brother in a single-parent home; they were supported and surrounded by extended family. The life lessons were timeless and valuable. Paula, like most, has had her challenges, but she remains faithful, understanding that her life is fueled by the power of God.

After being married for thirty-three years, Paula is adjusting to life as a widow. Together, she and her husband raised three children while serving in various ministries at church and in their community. They enjoyed music and annual road trips with their children.

Paula loves working with people, and she is most energized when helping others identify and reach their goals. While writing '*Walk Into Your New*,' Paula noted that we must remain intentional and purposeful about our living. She hopes to pass this on to others through her writings and work as a Life Coach and Consultant.

Visit my Website: www.livinonpurpose.com to purchase additional copies of "**Walk Into Your New: Transitioning from Mourning to Joy**" and promotional items.

**Telephone 609-232-2723**

**Email: panderson@livinonpurpose.com**

CPSIA information can be obtained
at www.ICGtesting.com
Printed in the USA
FSHW021632080222